Fruit & Vegetable
Garden Notes

This Notebook Belongs To:

....

....

....

....

FRUIT & VEGETABLE
GARDEN NOTES

CICO BOOKS
LONDON NEW YORK

Published in 2013 by CICO Books
An imprint of Ryland Peters & Small Ltd
20–21 Jockey's Fields   519 Broadway, 5th Floor
London WC1R 4BW   New York, NY 10012

www.cicobooks.com

10 9 8 7 6 5 4 3 2 1

Compilation © CICO Books 2013
Design and illustration © CICO Books 2013

A CIP catalog record for this book is available from
the Library of Congress and the British Library.

ISBN: 978 1 908862 85 3

Design: Jerry Goldie
Motif illustration: Jane Smith

Style photography: David Merewether except page 10
by Lucinda Symons and page 11 by Caroline Hughes

Printed in China

For digital editions, visit
www.cicobooks.com/apps.php

CONTENTS

GETTING STARTED

TOMATO

JOHN BAER
POMEDORO GROSSO

CARD SEED.CO.
FREDONIA, N.Y.

WHAT TO GROW

Depending on where you live, there are hundreds of different vegetables, fruits, and herbs in just as many varieties. Try experimenting—you will soon find out what suits your soil, your climate, and your patience. To avoid gluts of the same foods, sow as wide a variety as possible, and try to plant crops that can be harvested at different times of the year. It is also wise to choose those vegetables and fruits that are expensive to buy, as well as the ones that you are particularly fond of.

The following can be grown successfully in the vegetable garden or allotment:

Vegetables
artichokes
asparagus
beets
bell peppers
borlotti beans
broccoli
Brussels sprouts
cabbages
carrots
cauliflower
celeriac
celery
corn
cucumbers

eggplants (aubergine)
fava (broad) beans
fennel
garlic
green beans
green (spring) onions
Jerusalem artichokes
kale
kohlrabi
leeks
lettuce
marrows
onions
parsnips
peas

pole lima beans
potatoes
pumpkins
radishes
rutabagas (swede)
scarlet-runner beans
shallots
sprouting broccoli
squash
sweet potatoes
tomatoes
turnips
zucchini (courgettes)

Fruit
blueberries
gooseberries
grapes
raspberries
red currants
rhubarb
strawberries
white currants

Herbs
basil
cilantro (coriander)
mint
oregano
parsley
rosemary
sage
tarragon
thyme

PLANNING YOUR PLOT

Use these grids to work out how you would like to lay out your plot. Consider factors such as how much space each plant will take up, crop rotation, companion planting, the direction of sunlight, and location of water supply.

NOTES

NOTES

VEGETABLES

PEAS
EARLY ALASKA

CARD SEED Co.
FREDONIA, N.Y.

RADISH
WHITE TIP SCARLET TURNIP

CARD SEED Co.
FREDONIA, N.Y.

ROOT VEGETABLES

Vegetable name:
....

Variety planted:
....

Seeds sown:
....

Germination period:
....

Seedlings planted out:
....

Harvest:
....
....

Comments:
....
....
....
....
....
....
....
....
....

Vegetable name:
....

Variety planted:
....

Seeds sown:
....

Germination period:
....

Seedlings planted out:
....

Harvest:
....
....

Comments:
....
....
....
....
....
....
....
....
....

Vegetable name:
....

Variety planted:
....

Seeds sown:
....

Germination period:
....

Seedlings planted out:
....

Harvest:
....
....

Comments:
....
....
....
....
....
....
....

Vegetable name:
....

Variety planted:
....

Seeds sown:
....

Germination period:
....

Seedlings planted out:
....

Harvest:
....
....

Comments:
....
....
....
....
....
....
....

Vegetable name:

Variety planted:

Seeds sown:

Germination period:

Seedlings planted out:

Harvest:

Comments:

Vegetable name:

Variety planted:

Seeds sown:

Germination period:

Seedlings planted out:

Harvest:

Comments:

Vegetable name:

Variety planted:

Seeds sown:

Germination period:

Seedlings planted out:

Harvest:

Comments:

Vegetable name:

Variety planted:

Seeds sown:

Germination period:

Seedlings planted out:

Harvest:

Comments:

ROOT VEGETABLES

Vegetable name:

Variety planted:

Seeds sown:

Germination period:

Seedlings planted out:

Harvest:

Comments:

Vegetable name:

Variety planted:

Seeds sown:

Germination period:

Seedlings planted out:

Harvest:

Comments:

Vegetable name:

Variety planted:

Seeds sown:

Germination period:

Seedlings planted out:

Harvest:

Comments:

Vegetable name:

Variety planted:

Seeds sown:

Germination period:

Seedlings planted out:

Harvest:

Comments:

Vegetable name:
....

Variety planted:
....

Seeds sown:
....

Germination period:
....

Seedlings planted out:
....

Harvest:
....
....

Comments:
....
....
....
....
....
....
....

Vegetable name:
....

Variety planted:
....

Seeds sown:
....

Germination period:
....

Seedlings planted out:
....

Harvest:
....
....

Comments:
....
....
....
....
....
....
....

Vegetable name:
....

Variety planted:
....

Seeds sown:
....

Germination period:
....

Seedlings planted out:
....

Harvest:
....
....

Comments:
....
....
....
....
....
....
....

Vegetable name:
....

Variety planted:
....

Seeds sown:
....

Germination period:
....

Seedlings planted out:
....

Harvest:
....
....

Comments:
....
....
....
....
....
....
....

Root Vegetables

Vegetable name:
....

Variety planted:
....

Seeds sown:
....

Germination period:
....

Seedlings planted out:
....

Harvest:
....

Comments:
....
....
....
....
....
....

Vegetable name:
....

Variety planted:
....

Seeds sown:
....

Germination period:
....

Seedlings planted out:
....

Harvest:
....

Comments:
....
....
....
....
....
....

Vegetable name:
....

Variety planted:
....

Seeds sown:
....

Germination period:
....

Seedlings planted out:
....

Harvest:
....

Comments:
....
....
....
....

Vegetable name:
....

Variety planted:
....

Seeds sown:
....

Germination period:
....

Seedlings planted out:
....

Harvest:
....

Comments:
....
....
....
....

Vegetable name:
....

Variety planted:
....

Seeds sown:
....

Germination period:
....

Seedlings planted out:
....

Harvest:
....

Comments:
....
....
....
....
....
....

Vegetable name:
....

Variety planted:
....

Seeds sown:
....

Germination period:
....

Seedlings planted out:
....

Harvest:
....

Comments:
....
....
....
....
....
....

Vegetable name:
....

Variety planted:
....

Seeds sown:
....

Germination period:
....

Seedlings planted out:
....

Harvest:
....

Comments:
....
....
....
....
....
....

Vegetable name:
....

Variety planted:
....

Seeds sown:
....

Germination period:
....

Seedlings planted out:
....

Harvest:
....

Comments:
....
....
....
....
....
....

ROOT VEGETABLES

Vegetable name:

Variety planted:

Seeds sown:

Germination period:

Seedlings planted out:

Harvest:

Comments:

Vegetable name:

Variety planted:

Seeds sown:

Germination period:

Seedlings planted out:

Harvest:

Comments:

Vegetable name:

Variety planted:

Seeds sown:

Germination period:

Seedlings planted out:

Harvest:

Comments:

Vegetable name:

Variety planted:

Seeds sown:

Germination period:

Seedlings planted out:

Harvest:

Comments:

Vegetable name:
....

Variety planted:
....
Seeds sown:
....
Germination period:
....
Seedlings planted out:
....
Harvest:
....

Comments:
....
....
....
....
....
....

Vegetable name:
....

Variety planted:
....
Seeds sown:
....
Germination period:
....
Seedlings planted out:
....
Harvest:
....

Comments:
....
....
....
....
....
....

Vegetable name:
....

Variety planted:
....
Seeds sown:
....
Germination period:
....
Seedlings planted out:
....
Harvest:
....

Comments:
....
....
....
....
....

Vegetable name:
....

Variety planted:
....
Seeds sown:
....
Germination period:
....
Seedlings planted out:
....
Harvest:
....

Comments:
....
....
....
....
....

ROOT VEGETABLES

Vegetable name: ....

Variety planted: ....

Seeds sown: ....

Germination period: ....

Seedlings planted out: ....

Harvest: ....

Comments: ....

....

....

....

....

....

Vegetable name: ....

Variety planted: ....

Seeds sown: ....

Germination period: ....

Seedlings planted out: ....

Harvest: ....

Comments: ....

....

....

....

....

....

Vegetable name: ....

Variety planted: ....

Seeds sown: ....

Germination period: ....

Seedlings planted out: ....

Harvest: ....

Comments: ....

....

....

....

....

....

Vegetable name: ....

Variety planted: ....

Seeds sown: ....

Germination period: ....

Seedlings planted out: ....

Harvest: ....

Comments: ....

....

....

....

....

....

Vegetable name:
....

Variety planted:
....

Seeds sown:
....

Germination period:
....

Seedlings planted out:
....

Harvest:
....

Comments:
....
....
....
....
....
....

Vegetable name:
....

Variety planted:
....

Seeds sown:
....

Germination period:
....

Seedlings planted out:
....

Harvest:
....

Comments:
....
....
....
....
....
....

Vegetable name:
....

Variety planted:
....

Seeds sown:
....

Germination period:
....

Seedlings planted out:
....

Harvest:
....

Comments:
....
....
....
....
....
....

Vegetable name:
....

Variety planted:
....

Seeds sown:
....

Germination period:
....

Seedlings planted out:
....

Harvest:
....

Comments:
....
....
....
....
....
....

Root Vegetables

Vegetable name:
....

Variety planted:
....

Seeds sown:
....

Germination period:
....

Seedlings planted out:
....

Harvest:
....

Comments:
....
....
....
....
....
....
....

Vegetable name:
....

Variety planted:
....

Seeds sown:
....

Germination period:
....

Seedlings planted out:
....

Harvest:
....

Comments:
....
....
....
....
....
....
....

Vegetable name:
....

Variety planted:
....

Seeds sown:
....

Germination period:
....

Seedlings planted out:
....

Harvest:
....

Comments:
....
....
....
....
....
....
....

Vegetable name:
....

Variety planted:
....

Seeds sown:
....

Germination period:
....

Seedlings planted out:
....

Harvest:
....

Comments:
....
....
....
....
....
....
....

Vegetable name:
....

Variety planted:
....

Seeds sown:
....

Germination period:
....

Seedlings planted out:
....

Harvest:
....

Comments:
....
....
....
....
....
....

Vegetable name:
....

Variety planted:
....

Seeds sown:
....

Germination period:
....

Seedlings planted out:
....

Harvest:
....

Comments:
....
....
....
....
....
....

Vegetable name:
....

Variety planted:
....

Seeds sown:
....

Germination period:
....

Seedlings planted out:
....

Harvest:
....

Comments:
....
....
....
....
....
....

Vegetable name:
....

Variety planted:
....

Seeds sown:
....

Germination period:
....

Seedlings planted out:
....

Harvest:
....

Comments:
....
....
....
....
....
....

SALAD LEAVES

Vegetable name:

Variety planted:

Seeds sown:

Germination period:

Seedlings planted out:

Harvest:

Comments:

Vegetable name:

Variety planted:

Seeds sown:

Germination period:

Seedlings planted out:

Harvest:

Comments:

Vegetable name:

Variety planted:

Seeds sown:

Germination period:

Seedlings planted out:

Harvest:

Comments:

Vegetable name:

Variety planted:

Seeds sown:

Germination period:

Seedlings planted out:

Harvest:

Comments:

Vegetable name:

Variety planted:

Seeds sown:

Germination period:

Seedlings planted out:

Harvest:

Comments:

Vegetable name:

Variety planted:

Seeds sown:

Germination period:

Seedlings planted out:

Harvest:

Comments:

Vegetable name:

Variety planted:

Seeds sown:

Germination period:

Seedlings planted out:

Harvest:

Comments:

Vegetable name:

Variety planted:

Seeds sown:

Germination period:

Seedlings planted out:

Harvest:

Comments:

Salad Leaves

Vegetable name:
....

Variety planted:
....

Seeds sown:
....

Germination period:
....

Seedlings planted out:
....

Harvest:
....

Comments:
....
....
....
....
....
....

Vegetable name:
....

Variety planted:
....

Seeds sown:
....

Germination period:
....

Seedlings planted out:
....

Harvest:
....

Comments:
....
....
....
....
....
....

Vegetable name:
....

Variety planted:
....

Seeds sown:
....

Germination period:
....

Seedlings planted out:
....

Harvest:
....

Comments:
....
....
....
....
....
....

Vegetable name:
....

Variety planted:
....

Seeds sown:
....

Germination period:
....

Seedlings planted out:
....

Harvest:
....

Comments:
....
....
....
....
....
....

Vegetable name:

Variety planted:

Seeds sown:

Germination period:

Seedlings planted out:

Harvest:

Comments:

Vegetable name:

Variety planted:

Seeds sown:

Germination period:

Seedlings planted out:

Harvest:

Comments:

Vegetable name:

Variety planted:

Seeds sown:

Germination period:

Seedlings planted out:

Harvest:

Comments:

Vegetable name:

Variety planted:

Seeds sown:

Germination period:

Seedlings planted out:

Harvest:

Comments:

SALAD LEAVES

Vegetable name:

Variety planted:

Seeds sown:

Germination period:

Seedlings planted out:

Harvest:

Comments:

Vegetable name:

Variety planted:

Seeds sown:

Germination period:

Seedlings planted out:

Harvest:

Comments:

Vegetable name:

Variety planted:

Seeds sown:

Germination period:

Seedlings planted out:

Harvest:

Comments:

Vegetable name:

Variety planted:

Seeds sown:

Germination period:

Seedlings planted out:

Harvest:

Comments:

Vegetable name:

Variety planted:

Seeds sown:

Germination period:

Seedlings planted out:

Harvest:

Comments:

Vegetable name:

Variety planted:

Seeds sown:

Germination period:

Seedlings planted out:

Harvest:

Comments:

Vegetable name:

Variety planted:

Seeds sown:

Germination period:

Seedlings planted out:

Harvest:

Comments:

Vegetable name:

Variety planted:

Seeds sown:

Germination period:

Seedlings planted out:

Harvest:

Comments:

SALAD LEAVES

Vegetable name:

Variety planted:

Seeds sown:

Germination period:

Seedlings planted out:

Harvest:

Comments:

Vegetable name:

Variety planted:

Seeds sown:

Germination period:

Seedlings planted out:

Harvest:

Comments:

Vegetable name:

Variety planted:

Seeds sown:

Germination period:

Seedlings planted out:

Harvest:

Comments:

Vegetable name:

Variety planted:

Seeds sown:

Germination period:

Seedlings planted out:

Harvest:

Comments:

Vegetable name:

Variety planted:

Seeds sown:

Germination period:

Seedlings planted out:

Harvest:

Comments:

Vegetable name:

Variety planted:

Seeds sown:

Germination period:

Seedlings planted out:

Harvest:

Comments:

Vegetable name:

Variety planted:

Seeds sown:

Germination period:

Seedlings planted out:

Harvest:

Comments:

Vegetable name:

Variety planted:

Seeds sown:

Germination period:

Seedlings planted out:

Harvest:

Comments:

SALAD LEAVES

Vegetable name:
....

Variety planted:
....

Seeds sown:
....

Germination period:
....

Seedlings planted out:
....

Harvest:
....

Comments:
....
....
....
....
....
....
....
....

Vegetable name:
....

Variety planted:
....

Seeds sown:
....

Germination period:
....

Seedlings planted out:
....

Harvest:
....

Comments:
....
....
....
....
....
....
....
....

Vegetable name:
....

Variety planted:
....

Seeds sown:
....

Germination period:
....

Seedlings planted out:
....

Harvest:
....

Comments:
....
....
....
....
....

Vegetable name:
....

Variety planted:
....

Seeds sown:
....

Germination period:
....

Seedlings planted out:
....

Harvest:
....

Comments:
....
....
....
....
....

Vegetable name:

Variety planted:

Seeds sown:

Germination period:

Seedlings planted out:

Harvest:

Comments:

Vegetable name:

Variety planted:

Seeds sown:

Germination period:

Seedlings planted out:

Harvest:

Comments:

Vegetable name:

Variety planted:

Seeds sown:

Germination period:

Seedlings planted out:

Harvest:

Comments:

Vegetable name:

Variety planted:

Seeds sown:

Germination period:

Seedlings planted out:

Harvest:

Comments:

SALAD LEAVES

Vegetable name:
....

Variety planted:
....

Seeds sown:
....

Germination period:
....

Seedlings planted out:
....

Harvest:
....

Comments:
....
....
....
....
....
....

Vegetable name:
....

Variety planted:
....

Seeds sown:
....

Germination period:
....

Seedlings planted out:
....

Harvest:
....

Comments:
....
....
....
....
....
....

Vegetable name:
....

Variety planted:
....

Seeds sown:
....

Germination period:
....

Seedlings planted out:
....

Harvest:
....

Comments:
....
....
....
....
....
....

Vegetable name:
....

Variety planted:
....

Seeds sown:
....

Germination period:
....

Seedlings planted out:
....

Harvest:
....

Comments:
....
....
....
....
....
....

Vegetable name:
....

Variety planted:
....

Seeds sown:
....

Germination period:
....

Seedlings planted out:
....

Harvest:
....

Comments:
....
....
....
....
....
....

Vegetable name:
....

Variety planted:
....

Seeds sown:
....

Germination period:
....

Seedlings planted out:
....

Harvest:
....

Comments:
....
....
....
....
....
....

Vegetable name:
....

Variety planted:
....

Seeds sown:
....

Germination period:
....

Seedlings planted out:
....

Harvest:
....

Comments:
....
....
....
....
....
....

Vegetable name:
....

Variety planted:
....

Seeds sown:
....

Germination period:
....

Seedlings planted out:
....

Harvest:
....

Comments:
....
....
....
....
....
....

Onion Family

Vegetable name:

Variety planted:

Seeds sown:

Germination period:

Seedlings planted out:

Harvest:

Comments:

Vegetable name:

Variety planted:

Seeds sown:

Germination period:

Seedlings planted out:

Harvest:

Comments:

Vegetable name:

Variety planted:

Seeds sown:

Germination period:

Seedlings planted out:

Harvest:

Comments:

Vegetable name:

Variety planted:

Seeds sown:

Germination period:

Seedlings planted out:

Harvest:

Comments:

Vegetable name:
....

Variety planted:
....

Seeds sown:
....

Germination period:
....

Seedlings planted out:
....

Harvest:
....

Comments:
....
....
....
....
....

Vegetable name:
....

Variety planted:
....

Seeds sown:
....

Germination period:
....

Seedlings planted out:
....

Harvest:
....

Comments:
....
....
....
....
....

Vegetable name:
....

Variety planted:
....

Seeds sown:
....

Germination period:
....

Seedlings planted out:
....

Harvest:
....

Comments:
....
....
....
....
....

Vegetable name:
....

Variety planted:
....

Seeds sown:
....

Germination period:
....

Seedlings planted out:
....

Harvest:
....

Comments:
....
....
....
....
....

ONION FAMILY

Vegetable name:
....

Variety planted:
....

Seeds sown:
....

Germination period:
....

Seedlings planted out:
....

Harvest:
....

Comments:
....
....
....
....
....
....

Vegetable name:
....

Variety planted:
....

Seeds sown:
....

Germination period:
....

Seedlings planted out:
....

Harvest:
....

Comments:
....
....
....
....
....
....

Vegetable name:
....

Variety planted:
....

Seeds sown:
....

Germination period:
....

Seedlings planted out:
....

Harvest:
....

Comments:
....
....
....
....
....
....

Vegetable name:
....

Variety planted:
....

Seeds sown:
....

Germination period:
....

Seedlings planted out:
....

Harvest:
....

Comments:
....
....
....
....
....
....

Vegetable name:
....
....

Variety planted:
....

Seeds sown:
....

Germination period:
....

Seedlings planted out:
....

Harvest:
....
....

Comments:
....
....
....
....
....
....

Vegetable name:
....
....

Variety planted:
....

Seeds sown:
....

Germination period:
....

Seedlings planted out:
....

Harvest:
....
....

Comments:
....
....
....
....
....
....

Vegetable name:
....
....

Variety planted:
....

Seeds sown:
....

Germination period:
....

Seedlings planted out:
....

Harvest:
....
....

Comments:
....
....
....
....
....
....

Vegetable name:
....
....

Variety planted:
....

Seeds sown:
....

Germination period:
....

Seedlings planted out:
....

Harvest:
....
....

Comments:
....
....
....
....
....
....

Onion Family

Vegetable name:

Variety planted:

Seeds sown:

Germination period:

Seedlings planted out:

Harvest:

Comments:

Vegetable name:

Variety planted:

Seeds sown:

Germination period:

Seedlings planted out:

Harvest:

Comments:

Vegetable name:

Variety planted:

Seeds sown:

Germination period:

Seedlings planted out:

Harvest:

Comments:

Vegetable name:

Variety planted:

Seeds sown:

Germination period:

Seedlings planted out:

Harvest:

Comments:

Vegetable name:
....

Variety planted:
....

Seeds sown:
....

Germination period:
....

Seedlings planted out:
....

Harvest:
....

Comments:
....
....
....
....
....
....

Vegetable name:
....

Variety planted:
....

Seeds sown:
....

Germination period:
....

Seedlings planted out:
....

Harvest:
....

Comments:
....
....
....
....
....
....

Vegetable name:
....

Variety planted:
....

Seeds sown:
....

Germination period:
....

Seedlings planted out:
....

Harvest:
....

Comments:
....
....
....
....
....
....

Vegetable name:
....

Variety planted:
....

Seeds sown:
....

Germination period:
....

Seedlings planted out:
....

Harvest:
....

Comments:
....
....
....
....
....
....

ONION FAMILY

Vegetable name:

Variety planted:

Seeds sown:

Germination period:

Seedlings planted out:

Harvest:

Comments:

Vegetable name:

Variety planted:

Seeds sown:

Germination period:

Seedlings planted out:

Harvest:

Comments:

Vegetable name:

Variety planted:

Seeds sown:

Germination period:

Seedlings planted out:

Harvest:

Comments:

Vegetable name:

Variety planted:

Seeds sown:

Germination period:

Seedlings planted out:

Harvest:

Comments:

Vegetable name:
....

Variety planted:
....

Seeds sown:
....

Germination period:
....

Seedlings planted out:
....

Harvest:
....

....

Comments:
....

....

....

....

....

....

Vegetable name:
....

Variety planted:
....

Seeds sown:
....

Germination period:
....

Seedlings planted out:
....

Harvest:
....

....

Comments:
....

....

....

....

....

....

Vegetable name:
....

Variety planted:
....

Seeds sown:
....

Germination period:
....

Seedlings planted out:
....

Harvest:
....

....

Comments:
....

....

....

....

....

Vegetable name:
....

Variety planted:
....

Seeds sown:
....

Germination period:
....

Seedlings planted out:
....

Harvest:
....

....

Comments:
....

....

....

....

....

Onion Family

Vegetable name:
....

Variety planted:

Seeds sown:

Germination period:

Seedlings planted out:

Harvest:
....

Comments:
....
....
....
....
....
....

Vegetable name:
....

Variety planted:

Seeds sown:

Germination period:

Seedlings planted out:

Harvest:
....

Comments:
....
....
....
....
....
....

Vegetable name:
....

Variety planted:

Seeds sown:

Germination period:

Seedlings planted out:

Harvest:
....

Comments:
....
....
....
....
....
....

Vegetable name:
....

Variety planted:

Seeds sown:

Germination period:

Seedlings planted out:

Harvest:
....

Comments:
....
....
....
....
....
....

Vegetable name:
....

Variety planted:
....

Seeds sown:
....

Germination period:
....

Seedlings planted out:
....

Harvest:
....

....

Comments:
....

....

....

....

....

....

Vegetable name:
....

Variety planted:
....

Seeds sown:
....

Germination period:
....

Seedlings planted out:
....

Harvest:
....

....

Comments:
....

....

....

Vegetable name:
....

Variety planted:
....

Seeds sown:
....

Germination period:
....

Seedlings planted out:
....

Harvest:
....

....

Comments:
....

....

....

....

....

Vegetable name:
....

Variety planted:
....

Seeds sown:
....

Germination period:
....

Seedlings planted out:
....

Harvest:
....

....

Comments:
....

....

....

....

....

Onion Family

Vegetable name:
....

....

Variety planted:
....

Seeds sown:
....

Germination period:
....

Seedlings planted out:
....

Harvest:
....

Comments:
....

....

....

....

....

....

Vegetable name:
....

....

Variety planted:
....

Seeds sown:
....

Germination period:
....

Seedlings planted out:
....

Harvest:
....

Comments:
....

....

....

....

....

....

Vegetable name:
....

....

Variety planted:
....

Seeds sown:
....

Germination period:
....

Seedlings planted out:
....

Harvest:
....

Comments:
....

....

....

....

....

Vegetable name:
....

....

Variety planted:
....

Seeds sown:
....

Germination period:
....

Seedlings planted out:
....

Harvest:
....

Comments:
....

....

....

....

....

Vegetable name:

Variety planted:

Seeds sown:

Germination period:

Seedlings planted out:

Harvest:

Comments:

Vegetable name:

Variety planted:

Seeds sown:

Germination period:

Seedlings planted out:

Harvest:

Comments:

Vegetable name:

Variety planted:

Seeds sown:

Germination period:

Seedlings planted out:

Harvest:

Comments:

Vegetable name:

Variety planted:

Seeds sown:

Germination period:

Seedlings planted out:

Harvest:

Comments:

TOMATOES

Vegetable name:
....

Variety planted:
Seeds sown:
Germination period:
Seedlings planted out:
Harvest:

Comments:
....
....
....
....

Vegetable name:
....

Variety planted:
Seeds sown:
Germination period:
Seedlings planted out:
Harvest:

Comments:
....
....
....
....

Vegetable name:
....

Variety planted:
Seeds sown:
Germination period:
Seedlings planted out:
Harvest:

Comments:
....
....
....
....

Vegetable name:
....

Variety planted:
Seeds sown:
Germination period:
Seedlings planted out:
Harvest:

Comments:
....
....
....
....

Vegetable name:

Variety planted:

Seeds sown:

Germination period:

Seedlings planted out:

Harvest:

Comments:

Vegetable name:

Variety planted:

Seeds sown:

Germination period:

Seedlings planted out:

Harvest:

Comments:

Vegetable name:

Variety planted:

Seeds sown:

Germination period:

Seedlings planted out:

Harvest:

Comments:

Vegetable name:

Variety planted:

Seeds sown:

Germination period:

Seedlings planted out:

Harvest:

Comments:

TOMATOES

Vegetable name:

Variety planted:

Seeds sown:

Germination period:

Seedlings planted out:

Harvest:

Comments:

Vegetable name:

Variety planted:

Seeds sown:

Germination period:

Seedlings planted out:

Harvest:

Comments:

Vegetable name:

Variety planted:

Seeds sown:

Germination period:

Seedlings planted out:

Harvest:

Comments:

Vegetable name:

Variety planted:

Seeds sown:

Germination period:

Seedlings planted out:

Harvest:

Comments:

Vegetable name:

Variety planted:

Seeds sown:

Germination period:

Seedlings planted out:

Harvest:

Comments:

Vegetable name:

Variety planted:

Seeds sown:

Germination period:

Seedlings planted out:

Harvest:

Comments:

Vegetable name:

Variety planted:

Seeds sown:

Germination period:

Seedlings planted out:

Harvest:

Comments:

Vegetable name:

Variety planted:

Seeds sown:

Germination period:

Seedlings planted out:

Harvest:

Comments:

TOMATOES

Vegetable name: ....

Variety planted: ....

Seeds sown: ....

Germination period: ....

Seedlings planted out: ....

Harvest: ....

Comments: ....

....

....

....

....

....

Vegetable name: ....

Variety planted: ....

Seeds sown: ....

Germination period: ....

Seedlings planted out: ....

Harvest: ....

Comments: ....

....

....

....

....

Vegetable name: ....

Variety planted: ....

Seeds sown: ....

Germination period: ....

Seedlings planted out: ....

Harvest: ....

Comments: ....

....

....

....

Vegetable name: ....

Variety planted: ....

Seeds sown: ....

Germination period: ....

Seedlings planted out: ....

Harvest: ....

Comments: ....

....

....

....

....

Vegetable name:

Variety planted:

Seeds sown:

Germination period:

Seedlings planted out:

Harvest:

Comments:

Vegetable name:

Variety planted:

Seeds sown:

Germination period:

Seedlings planted out:

Harvest:

Comments:

Vegetable name:

Variety planted:

Seeds sown:

Germination period:

Seedlings planted out:

Harvest:

Comments:

Vegetable name:

Variety planted:

Seeds sown:

Germination period:

Seedlings planted out:

Harvest:

Comments:

TOMATOES

Vegetable name:

Variety planted:

Seeds sown:

Germination period:

Seedlings planted out:

Harvest:

Comments:

Vegetable name:

Variety planted:

Seeds sown:

Germination period:

Seedlings planted out:

Harvest:

Comments:

Vegetable name:

Variety planted:

Seeds sown:

Germination period:

Seedlings planted out:

Harvest:

Comments:

Vegetable name:

Variety planted:

Seeds sown:

Germination period:

Seedlings planted out:

Harvest:

Comments:

Vegetable name:
....

Variety planted:

Seeds sown:

Germination period:

Seedlings planted out:

Harvest:

Comments:

Vegetable name:
....

Variety planted:

Seeds sown:

Germination period:

Seedlings planted out:

Harvest:

Comments:

Vegetable name:
....

Variety planted:

Seeds sown:

Germination period:

Seedlings planted out:

Harvest:

Comments:

Vegetable name:
....

Variety planted:

Seeds sown:

Germination period:

Seedlings planted out:

Harvest:

Comments:

TOMATOES

Vegetable name:

Variety planted:

Seeds sown:

Germination period:

Seedlings planted out:

Harvest:

Comments:

Vegetable name:

Variety planted:

Seeds sown:

Germination period:

Seedlings planted out:

Harvest:

Comments:

Vegetable name:

Variety planted:

Seeds sown:

Germination period:

Seedlings planted out:

Harvest:

Comments:

Vegetable name:

Variety planted:

Seeds sown:

Germination period:

Seedlings planted out:

Harvest:

Comments:

Vegetable name:

Variety planted:

Seeds sown:

Germination period:

Seedlings planted out:

Harvest:

Comments:

Vegetable name:

Variety planted:

Seeds sown:

Germination period:

Seedlings planted out:

Harvest:

Comments:

Vegetable name:

Variety planted:

Seeds sown:

Germination period:

Seedlings planted out:

Harvest:

Comments:

Vegetable name:

Variety planted:

Seeds sown:

Germination period:

Seedlings planted out:

Harvest:

Comments:

TOMATOES

Vegetable name:

Variety planted:

Seeds sown:

Germination period:

Seedlings planted out:

Harvest:

Comments:

Vegetable name:

Variety planted:

Seeds sown:

Germination period:

Seedlings planted out:

Harvest:

Comments:

Vegetable name:

Variety planted:

Seeds sown:

Germination period:

Seedlings planted out:

Harvest:

Comments:

Vegetable name:

Variety planted:

Seeds sown:

Germination period:

Seedlings planted out:

Harvest:

Comments:

Vegetable name:

Variety planted:

Seeds sown:

Germination period:

Seedlings planted out:

Harvest:

Comments:

Vegetable name:

Variety planted:

Seeds sown:

Germination period:

Seedlings planted out:

Harvest:

Comments:

Vegetable name:

Variety planted:

Seeds sown:

Germination period:

Seedlings planted out:

Harvest:

Comments:

Vegetable name:

Variety planted:

Seeds sown:

Germination period:

Seedlings planted out:

Harvest:

Comments:

BRASSICAS

Vegetable name:

Variety planted:

Seeds sown:

Germination period:

Seedlings planted out:

Harvest:

Comments:

Vegetable name:

Variety planted:

Seeds sown:

Germination period:

Seedlings planted out:

Harvest:

Comments:

Vegetable name:

Variety planted:

Seeds sown:

Germination period:

Seedlings planted out:

Harvest:

Comments:

Vegetable name:

Variety planted:

Seeds sown:

Germination period:

Seedlings planted out:

Harvest:

Comments:

Vegetable name:
....

Variety planted:
Seeds sown:
Germination period:
Seedlings planted out:
Harvest:

Comments:
....
....
....
....
....
....

Vegetable name:
....

Variety planted:
Seeds sown:
Germination period:
Seedlings planted out:
Harvest:

Comments:
....
....
....
....
....
....

Vegetable name:
....

Variety planted:
Seeds sown:
Germination period:
Seedlings planted out:
Harvest:

Comments:
....
....
....
....
....
....

Vegetable name:
....

Variety planted:
Seeds sown:
Germination period:
Seedlings planted out:
Harvest:

Comments:
....
....
....
....
....
....

Brassicas

Vegetable name:
....

Variety planted:
....

Seeds sown:
....

Germination period:
....

Seedlings planted out:
....

Harvest:
....

Comments:
....
....
....
....
....
....

Vegetable name:
....

Variety planted:
....

Seeds sown:
....

Germination period:
....

Seedlings planted out:
....

Harvest:
....

Comments:
....
....
....
....
....
....

Vegetable name:
....

Variety planted:
....

Seeds sown:
....

Germination period:
....

Seedlings planted out:
....

Harvest:
....

Comments:
....
....
....
....
....
....

Vegetable name:
....

Variety planted:
....

Seeds sown:
....

Germination period:
....

Seedlings planted out:
....

Harvest:
....

Comments:
....
....
....
....
....
....

Vegetable name:

Variety planted:

Seeds sown:

Germination period:

Seedlings planted out:

Harvest:

Comments:

Vegetable name:

Variety planted:

Seeds sown:

Germination period:

Seedlings planted out:

Harvest:

Comments:

Vegetable name:

Variety planted:

Seeds sown:

Germination period:

Seedlings planted out:

Harvest:

Comments:

Vegetable name:

Variety planted:

Seeds sown:

Germination period:

Seedlings planted out:

Harvest:

Comments:

BRASSICAS

Vegetable name:
....

Variety planted:
....

Seeds sown:
....

Germination period:
....

Seedlings planted out:
....

Harvest:
....

Comments:
....
....
....
....
....
....

Vegetable name:
....

Variety planted:
....

Seeds sown:
....

Germination period:
....

Seedlings planted out:
....

Harvest:
....

Comments:
....
....
....
....
....
....

Vegetable name:
....

Variety planted:
....

Seeds sown:
....

Germination period:
....

Seedlings planted out:
....

Harvest:
....

Comments:
....
....
....
....
....
....

Vegetable name:
....

Variety planted:
....

Seeds sown:
....

Germination period:
....

Seedlings planted out:
....

Harvest:
....

Comments:
....
....
....
....
....
....

Vegetable name:
....

Variety planted:
Seeds sown:
Germination period:
Seedlings planted out:
Harvest:

Comments:
....
....
....
....
....

Vegetable name:
....

Variety planted:
Seeds sown:
Germination period:
Seedlings planted out:
Harvest:

Comments:
....
....
....

Vegetable name:
....

Variety planted:
Seeds sown:
Germination period:
Seedlings planted out:
Harvest:

Comments:
....
....
....
....
....

Vegetable name:
....

Variety planted:
Seeds sown:
Germination period:
Seedlings planted out:
Harvest:

Comments:
....
....
....
....
....

BRASSICAS

Vegetable name:
....

Variety planted:
....

Seeds sown:
....

Germination period:
....

Seedlings planted out:
....

Harvest:
....

Comments:
....
....
....
....
....
....

Vegetable name:
....

Variety planted:
....

Seeds sown:
....

Germination period:
....

Seedlings planted out:
....

Harvest:
....

Comments:
....
....
....
....
....
....

Vegetable name:
....

Variety planted:
....

Seeds sown:
....

Germination period:
....

Seedlings planted out:
....

Harvest:
....

Comments:
....
....
....
....
....
....

Vegetable name:
....

Variety planted:
....

Seeds sown:
....

Germination period:
....

Seedlings planted out:
....

Harvest:
....

Comments:
....
....
....
....
....
....

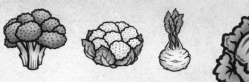

Vegetable name:
....

Variety planted:
....

Seeds sown:
....

Germination period:
....

Seedlings planted out:
....

Harvest:
....

Comments:
....
....
....
....
....
....

Vegetable name:
....

Variety planted:
....

Seeds sown:
....

Germination period:
....

Seedlings planted out:
....

Harvest:
....

Comments:
....
....
....
....
....
....

Vegetable name:
....

Variety planted:
....

Seeds sown:
....

Germination period:
....

Seedlings planted out:
....

Harvest:
....

Comments:
....
....
....
....
....
....

Vegetable name:
....

Variety planted:
....

Seeds sown:
....

Germination period:
....

Seedlings planted out:
....

Harvest:
....

Comments:
....
....
....
....
....
....

BRASSICAS

Vegetable name:

Variety planted:

Seeds sown:

Germination period:

Seedlings planted out:

Harvest:

Comments:

Vegetable name:

Variety planted:

Seeds sown:

Germination period:

Seedlings planted out:

Harvest:

Comments:

Vegetable name:

Variety planted:

Seeds sown:

Germination period:

Seedlings planted out:

Harvest:

Comments:

Vegetable name:

Variety planted:

Seeds sown:

Germination period:

Seedlings planted out:

Harvest:

Comments:

Vegetable name:

Variety planted:

Seeds sown:

Germination period:

Seedlings planted out:

Harvest:

Comments:

Vegetable name:

Variety planted:

Seeds sown:

Germination period:

Seedlings planted out:

Harvest:

Comments:

Vegetable name:

Variety planted:

Seeds sown:

Germination period:

Seedlings planted out:

Harvest:

Comments:

Vegetable name:

Variety planted:

Seeds sown:

Germination period:

Seedlings planted out:

Harvest:

Comments:

BRASSICAS

Vegetable name:

Variety planted:

Seeds sown:

Germination period:

Seedlings planted out:

Harvest:

Comments:

Vegetable name:

Variety planted:

Seeds sown:

Germination period:

Seedlings planted out:

Harvest:

Comments:

Vegetable name:

Variety planted:

Seeds sown:

Germination period:

Seedlings planted out:

Harvest:

Comments:

Vegetable name:

Variety planted:

Seeds sown:

Germination period:

Seedlings planted out:

Harvest:

Comments:

Vegetable name:
....

Variety planted:
....

Seeds sown:
....

Germination period:
....

Seedlings planted out:
....

Harvest:
....

Comments:
....
....
....
....
....
....

Vegetable name:
....

Variety planted:
....

Seeds sown:
....

Germination period:
....

Seedlings planted out:
....

Harvest:
....

Comments:
....
....
....
....
....
....

Vegetable name:
....

Variety planted:
....

Seeds sown:
....

Germination period:
....

Seedlings planted out:
....

Harvest:
....

Comments:
....
....
....
....
....
....

Vegetable name:
....

Variety planted:
....

Seeds sown:
....

Germination period:
....

Seedlings planted out:
....

Harvest:
....

Comments:
....
....
....
....
....
....

LEGUMES AND OTHER VEGETABLES

Vegetable name:

Variety planted:

Seeds sown:

Germination period:

Seedlings planted out:

Harvest:

Comments:

Vegetable name:

Variety planted:

Seeds sown:

Germination period:

Seedlings planted out:

Harvest:

Comments:

Vegetable name:

Variety planted:

Seeds sown:

Germination period:

Seedlings planted out:

Harvest:

Comments:

Vegetable name:

Variety planted:

Seeds sown:

Germination period:

Seedlings planted out:

Harvest:

Comments:

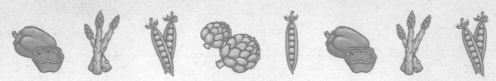

Vegetable name:
....

Variety planted:
....

Seeds sown:
....

Germination period:
....

Seedlings planted out:
....

Harvest:
....

....

Comments:
....

....

....

....

....

....

....

Vegetable name:
....

Variety planted:
....

Seeds sown:
....

Germination period:
....

Seedlings planted out:
....

Harvest:
....

....

Comments:
....

....

....

....

....

....

Vegetable name:
....

Variety planted:
....

Seeds sown:
....

Germination period:
....

Seedlings planted out:
....

Harvest:
....

....

Comments:
....

....

....

....

....

....

Vegetable name:
....

Variety planted:
....

Seeds sown:
....

Germination period:
....

Seedlings planted out:
....

Harvest:
....

....

Comments:
....

....

....

....

....

....

LEGUMES AND OTHER VEGETABLES

Vegetable name:
....

Variety planted:
....

Seeds sown:
....

Germination period:
....

Seedlings planted out:
....

Harvest:
....

Comments:
....
....
....
....
....
....

Vegetable name:
....

Variety planted:
....

Seeds sown:
....

Germination period:
....

Seedlings planted out:
....

Harvest:
....

Comments:
....
....
....
....
....
....

Vegetable name:
....

Variety planted:
....

Seeds sown:
....

Germination period:
....

Seedlings planted out:
....

Harvest:
....

Comments:
....
....
....
....
....
....

Vegetable name:
....

Variety planted:
....

Seeds sown:
....

Germination period:
....

Seedlings planted out:
....

Harvest:
....

Comments:
....
....
....
....
....
....

Vegetable name:

Variety planted:

Seeds sown:

Germination period:

Seedlings planted out:

Harvest:

Comments:

Vegetable name:

Variety planted:

Seeds sown:

Germination period:

Seedlings planted out:

Harvest:

Comments:

Vegetable name:

Variety planted:

Seeds sown:

Germination period:

Seedlings planted out:

Harvest:

Comments:

Vegetable name:

Variety planted:

Seeds sown:

Germination period:

Seedlings planted out:

Harvest:

Comments:

LEGUMES AND OTHER VEGETABLES

Vegetable name:
....

Variety planted:
....

Seeds sown:
....

Germination period:
....

Seedlings planted out:
....

Harvest:
....

Comments:
....
....
....
....
....

Vegetable name:
....

Variety planted:
....

Seeds sown:
....

Germination period:
....

Seedlings planted out:
....

Harvest:
....

Comments:
....
....
....
....
....

Vegetable name:
....

Variety planted:
....

Seeds sown:
....

Germination period:
....

Seedlings planted out:
....

Harvest:
....

Comments:
....
....
....
....

Vegetable name:
....

Variety planted:
....

Seeds sown:
....

Germination period:
....

Seedlings planted out:
....

Harvest:
....

Comments:
....
....
....

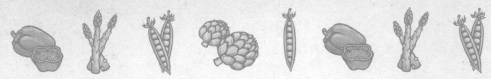

Vegetable name:

Variety planted:

Seeds sown:

Germination period:

Seedlings planted out:

Harvest:

Comments:

Vegetable name:

Variety planted:

Seeds sown:

Germination period:

Seedlings planted out:

Harvest:

Comments:

Vegetable name:

Variety planted:

Seeds sown:

Germination period:

Seedlings planted out:

Harvest:

Comments:

Vegetable name:

Variety planted:

Seeds sown:

Germination period:

Seedlings planted out:

Harvest:

Comments:

LEGUMES AND OTHER VEGETABLES

Vegetable name: ....

Variety planted: ....

Seeds sown: ....

Germination period: ....

Seedlings planted out: ....

Harvest: ....

Comments: ....

....

....

....

....

....

Vegetable name: ....

Variety planted: ....

Seeds sown: ....

Germination period: ....

Seedlings planted out: ....

Harvest: ....

Comments: ....

....

....

....

....

....

Vegetable name: ....

Variety planted: ....

Seeds sown: ....

Germination period: ....

Seedlings planted out: ....

Harvest: ....

Comments: ....

....

....

....

....

....

Vegetable name: ....

Variety planted: ....

Seeds sown: ....

Germination period: ....

Seedlings planted out: ....

Harvest: ....

Comments: ....

....

....

....

....

....

Vegetable name:
....

Variety planted:
....

Seeds sown:
....

Germination period:
....

Seedlings planted out:
....

Harvest:
....

....

Comments:
....

....

....

....

....

....

Vegetable name:
....

Variety planted:
....

Seeds sown:
....

Germination period:
....

Seedlings planted out:
....

Harvest:
....

....

Comments:
....

....

....

....

....

....

Vegetable name:
....

Variety planted:
....

Seeds sown:
....

Germination period:
....

Seedlings planted out:
....

Harvest:
....

....

Comments:
....

....

....

....

....

....

Vegetable name:
....

Variety planted:
....

Seeds sown:
....

Germination period:
....

Seedlings planted out:
....

Harvest:
....

....

Comments:
....

....

....

....

....

....

LEGUMES AND OTHER VEGETABLES

Vegetable name:

Variety planted:

Seeds sown:

Germination period:

Seedlings planted out:

Harvest:

Comments:

Vegetable name:

Variety planted:

Seeds sown:

Germination period:

Seedlings planted out:

Harvest:

Comments:

Vegetable name:

Variety planted:

Seeds sown:

Germination period:

Seedlings planted out:

Harvest:

Comments:

Vegetable name:

Variety planted:

Seeds sown:

Germination period:

Seedlings planted out:

Harvest:

Comments:

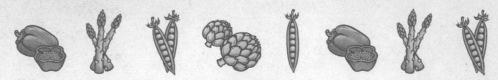

Vegetable name:
....

Variety planted:
....

Seeds sown:
....

Germination period:
....

Seedlings planted out:
....

Harvest:
....

Comments:
....
....
....
....
....
....

Vegetable name:
....

Variety planted:
....

Seeds sown:
....

Germination period:
....

Seedlings planted out:
....

Harvest:
....

Comments:
....

Vegetable name:
....

Variety planted:
....

Seeds sown:
....

Germination period:
....

Seedlings planted out:
....

Harvest:
....

Comments:
....
....
....
....

Vegetable name:
....

Variety planted:
....

Seeds sown:
....

Germination period:
....

Seedlings planted out:
....

Harvest:
....

Comments:
....
....
....
....

Legumes and Other Vegetables

Vegetable name:
....

Variety planted:
....

Seeds sown:
....

Germination period:
....

Seedlings planted out:
....

Harvest:
....

Comments:
....
....
....
....
....
....

Vegetable name:
....

Variety planted:
....

Seeds sown:
....

Germination period:
....

Seedlings planted out:
....

Harvest:
....

Comments:
....
....
....
....
....
....

Vegetable name:
....

Variety planted:
....

Seeds sown:
....

Germination period:
....

Seedlings planted out:
....

Harvest:
....

Comments:
....
....
....
....
....
....

Vegetable name:
....

Variety planted:
....

Seeds sown:
....

Germination period:
....

Seedlings planted out:
....

Harvest:
....

Comments:
....
....
....
....
....
....

Vegetable name:
....

Variety planted:
....

Seeds sown:
....

Germination period:
....

Seedlings planted out:
....

Harvest:
....

Comments:
....
....
....
....
....
....

Vegetable name:
....

Variety planted:
....

Seeds sown:
....

Germination period:
....

Seedlings planted out:
....

Harvest:
....

Comments:
....
....
....
....
....
....

Vegetable name:
....

Variety planted:
....

Seeds sown:
....

Germination period:
....

Seedlings planted out:
....

Harvest:
....

Comments:
....
....
....
....
....
....

Vegetable name:
....

Variety planted:
....

Seeds sown:
....

Germination period:
....

Seedlings planted out:
....

Harvest:
....

Comments:
....
....
....
....
....
....

NOTES

NOTES

NOTES

FRUIT

TREE FRUIT

Fruit name:
....

Variety planted:
....

Pruning:
....
....

Harvest:
....
....

Comments:
....
....
....
....
....
....
....
....

Fruit name:
....

Variety planted:
....

Pruning:
....
....

Harvest:
....
....

Comments:
....
....
....
....
....
....
....
....

Fruit name:
....

Variety planted:
....

Pruning:
....
....

Harvest:
....
....

Comments:
....
....
....
....
....
....
....
....

Fruit name:
....

Variety planted:
....

Pruning:
....
....

Harvest:
....
....

Comments:
....
....
....
....
....
....
....
....

Fruit name:
....

Variety planted:
....

Pruning:
....
....

Harvest:
....
....

Comments:
....
....
....
....
....
....
....
....

Fruit name:
....

Variety planted:
....

Pruning:
....
....

Harvest:
....
....

Comments:
....
....
....
....
....
....
....
....

Fruit name:
....

Variety planted:
....

Pruning:
....
....

Harvest:
....
....

Comments:
....
....
....
....
....
....
....
....

Fruit name:
....

Variety planted:
....

Pruning:
....
....

Harvest:
....
....

Comments:
....
....
....
....
....
....
....
....

TREE FRUIT

Fruit name:

Variety planted:

Pruning:

Harvest:

Comments:

Fruit name:

Variety planted:

Pruning:

Harvest:

Comments:

Fruit name:

Variety planted:

Pruning:

Harvest:

Comments:

Fruit name:

Variety planted:

Pruning:

Harvest:

Comments:

Fruit name:

Variety planted:

Pruning:

Harvest:

Comments:

Fruit name:

Variety planted:

Pruning:

Harvest:

Comments:

Fruit name:

Variety planted:

Pruning:

Harvest:

Comments:

Fruit name:

Variety planted:

Pruning:

Harvest:

Comments:

TREE FRUIT

Fruit name:

Variety planted:

Pruning:

Harvest:

Comments:

Fruit name:

Variety planted:

Pruning:

Harvest:

Comments:

Fruit name:

Variety planted:

Pruning:

Harvest:

Comments:

Fruit name:

Variety planted:

Pruning:

Harvest:

Comments:

Fruit name:

Variety planted:

Pruning:

Harvest:

Comments:

Fruit name:

Variety planted:

Pruning:

Harvest:

Comments:

Fruit name:

Variety planted:

Pruning:

Harvest:

Comments:

Fruit name:

Variety planted:

Pruning:

Harvest:

Comments:

TREE FRUIT

Fruit name:
....

Variety planted:
....

Pruning:
....
....

Harvest:
....
....

Comments:
....
....
....
....
....
....
....
....

Fruit name:
....

Variety planted:
....

Pruning:
....
....

Harvest:
....
....

Comments:
....
....
....
....
....
....
....
....

Fruit name:
....

Variety planted:
....

Pruning:
....
....

Harvest:
....
....

Comments:
....
....
....
....
....
....
....

Fruit name:
....

Variety planted:
....

Pruning:
....
....

Harvest:
....
....

Comments:
....
....
....
....
....
....
....

Fruit name:

Variety planted:

Pruning:

Harvest:

Comments:

Fruit name:

Variety planted:

Pruning:

Harvest:

Comments:

Fruit name:

Variety planted:

Pruning:

Harvest:

Comments:

Fruit name:

Variety planted:

Pruning:

Harvest:

Comments:

TREE FRUIT

Fruit name:

Variety planted:

Pruning:

Harvest:

Comments:

Fruit name:

Variety planted:

Pruning:

Harvest:

Comments:

Fruit name:

Variety planted:

Pruning:

Harvest:

Comments:

Fruit name:

Variety planted:

Pruning:

Harvest:

Comments:

Fruit name:

Variety planted:

Pruning:

Harvest:

Comments:

Fruit name:

Variety planted:

Pruning:

Harvest:

Comments:

Fruit name:

Variety planted:

Pruning:

Harvest:

Comments:

Fruit name:

Variety planted:

Pruning:

Harvest:

Comments:

BUSH FRUIT

Fruit name:

Variety planted:

Pruning:

Harvest:

Comments:

Fruit name:

Variety planted:

Pruning:

Harvest:

Comments:

Fruit name:

Variety planted:

Pruning:

Harvest:

Comments:

Fruit name:

Variety planted:

Pruning:

Harvest:

Comments:

Fruit name:

Variety planted:

Pruning:

Harvest:

Comments:

Fruit name:

Variety planted:

Pruning:

Harvest:

Comments:

Fruit name:

Variety planted:

Pruning:

Harvest:

Comments:

Fruit name:

Variety planted:

Pruning:

Harvest:

Comments:

BUSH FRUIT

Fruit name:

Variety planted:

Pruning:

Harvest:

Comments:

Fruit name:

Variety planted:

Pruning:

Harvest:

Comments:

Fruit name:

Variety planted:

Pruning:

Harvest:

Comments:

Fruit name:

Variety planted:

Pruning:

Harvest:

Comments:

Fruit name: ....

Variety planted: ....

Pruning: ....

....

Harvest: ....

....

Comments: ....

....

....

....

....

....

....

....

Fruit name: ....

Variety planted: ....

Pruning: ....

....

Harvest: ....

....

Comments: ....

....

....

....

....

....

....

....

Fruit name: ....

Variety planted: ....

Pruning: ....

....

Harvest: ....

....

Comments: ....

....

....

....

....

....

....

Fruit name: ....

Variety planted: ....

Pruning: ....

....

Harvest: ....

....

Comments: ....

....

....

....

....

....

....

BUSH FRUIT

Fruit name:

Variety planted:

Pruning:

Harvest:

Comments:

Fruit name:

Variety planted:

Pruning:

Harvest:

Comments:

Fruit name:

Variety planted:

Pruning:

Harvest:

Comments:

Fruit name:

Variety planted:

Pruning:

Harvest:

Comments:

Fruit name:
....

Variety planted:
....

Pruning:
....
....

Harvest:
....
....

Comments:
....
....
....
....
....
....
....
....

Fruit name:
....

Variety planted:
....

Pruning:
....
....

Harvest:
....
....

Comments:
....
....
....
....
....

Fruit name:
....

Variety planted:
....

Pruning:
....
....

Harvest:
....
....

Comments:
....
....
....
....
....
....
....

Fruit name:
....

Variety planted:
....

Pruning:
....
....

Harvest:
....
....

Comments:
....
....
....
....
....
....
....

BUSH FRUIT

Fruit name:

Variety planted:

Pruning:

Harvest:

Comments:

Fruit name:

Variety planted:

Pruning:

Harvest:

Comments:

Fruit name:

Variety planted:

Pruning:

Harvest:

Comments:

Fruit name:

Variety planted:

Pruning:

Harvest:

Comments:

Fruit name:
....

Variety planted:
....

Pruning:
....
....

Harvest:
....
....

Comments:
....
....
....
....
....
....
....
....

Fruit name:
....

Variety planted:
....

Pruning:
....
....

Harvest:
....
....

Comments:
....
....
....
....
....
....
....
....

Fruit name:
....

Variety planted:
....

Pruning:
....
....

Harvest:
....
....

Comments:
....
....
....
....
....
....
....

Fruit name:
....

Variety planted:
....

Pruning:
....
....

Harvest:
....
....

Comments:
....
....
....
....
....
....
....

BUSH FRUIT

Fruit name:

Variety planted:

Pruning:

Harvest:

Comments:

Fruit name:

Variety planted:

Pruning:

Harvest:

Comments:

Fruit name:

Variety planted:

Pruning:

Harvest:

Comments:

Fruit name:

Variety planted:

Pruning:

Harvest:

Comments:

Fruit name:

Variety planted:

Pruning:

Harvest:

Comments:

Fruit name:

Variety planted:

Pruning:

Harvest:

Comments:

Fruit name:

Variety planted:

Pruning:

Harvest:

Comments:

Fruit name:

Variety planted:

Pruning:

Harvest:

Comments:

NOTES

NOTES

NOTES

HERBS

Herb name:
....

Variety planted:
....

Seeds sown:
....

Germination period:
....

Seedlings planted out:
....

Harvest:
....

Successful varieties:
....

Comments:
....
....
....
....
....
....

Herb name:
....

Variety planted:
....

Seeds sown:
....

Germination period:
....

Seedlings planted out:
....

Harvest:
....

Successful varieties:
....

Comments:
....
....
....

Herb name:
....

Variety planted:
....

Seeds sown:
....

Germination period:
....

Seedlings planted out:
....

Harvest:
....

Successful varieties:
....

Comments:
....
....
....
....
....
....

Herb name:
....

Variety planted:
....

Seeds sown:
....

Germination period:
....

Seedlings planted out:
....

Harvest:
....

Successful varieties:
....

Comments:
....
....
....

Herb name:

Variety planted:

Seeds sown:

Germination period:

Seedlings planted out:

Harvest:

Successful varieties:

Comments:

Herb name:

Variety planted:

Seeds sown:

Germination period:

Seedlings planted out:

Harvest:

Successful varieties:

Comments:

Herb name:

Variety planted:

Seeds sown:

Germination period:

Seedlings planted out:

Harvest:

Successful varieties:

Comments:

Herb name:

Variety planted:

Seeds sown:

Germination period:

Seedlings planted out:

Harvest:

Successful varieties:

Comments:

Herbs

Herb name:
....

Variety planted:
Seeds sown:
Germination period:
Seedlings planted out:
Harvest:
Successful varieties:

Comments:

Herb name:
....

Variety planted:
Seeds sown:
Germination period:
Seedlings planted out:
Harvest:
Successful varieties:

Comments:

Herb name:
....

Variety planted:
Seeds sown:
Germination period:
Seedlings planted out:
Harvest:
Successful varieties:

Comments:

Herb name:
....

Variety planted:
Seeds sown:
Germination period:
Seedlings planted out:
Harvest:
Successful varieties:

Comments:

Herb name:
....

Variety planted:
....
Seeds sown:
....
Germination period:
....
Seedlings planted out:
....
Harvest:
....
Successful varieties:
....

Comments:
....
....
....
....
....
....

Herb name:
....

Variety planted:
....
Seeds sown:
....
Germination period:
....
Seedlings planted out:
....
Harvest:
....
Successful varieties:
....

Comments:
....
....
....
....
....
....

Herb name:
....

Variety planted:
....
Seeds sown:
....
Germination period:
....
Seedlings planted out:
....
Harvest:
....
Successful varieties:
....

Comments:
....
....
....
....
....
....

Herb name:
....

Variety planted:
....
Seeds sown:
....
Germination period:
....
Seedlings planted out:
....
Harvest:
....
Successful varieties:
....

Comments:
....
....
....
....
....
....

HERBS

Herb name:

Variety planted:

Seeds sown:

Germination period:

Seedlings planted out:

Harvest:

Successful varieties:

Comments:

Herb name:

Variety planted:

Seeds sown:

Germination period:

Seedlings planted out:

Harvest:

Successful varieties:

Comments:

Herb name:

Variety planted:

Seeds sown:

Germination period:

Seedlings planted out:

Harvest:

Successful varieties:

Comments:

Herb name:

Variety planted:

Seeds sown:

Germination period:

Seedlings planted out:

Harvest:

Successful varieties:

Comments:

Herb name:

Variety planted:

Seeds sown:

Germination period:

Seedlings planted out:

Harvest:

Successful varieties:

Comments:

Herb name:

Variety planted:

Seeds sown:

Germination period:

Seedlings planted out:

Harvest:

Successful varieties:

Comments:

Herb name:

Variety planted:

Seeds sown:

Germination period:

Seedlings planted out:

Harvest:

Successful varieties:

Comments:

Herb name:

Variety planted:

Seeds sown:

Germination period:

Seedlings planted out:

Harvest:

Successful varieties:

Comments:

HERBS

Herb name:

Variety planted:

Seeds sown:

Germination period:

Seedlings planted out:

Harvest:

Successful varieties:

Comments:

Herb name:

Variety planted:

Seeds sown:

Germination period:

Seedlings planted out:

Harvest:

Successful varieties:

Comments:

Herb name:

Variety planted:

Seeds sown:

Germination period:

Seedlings planted out:

Harvest:

Successful varieties:

Comments:

Herb name:

Variety planted:

Seeds sown:

Germination period:

Seedlings planted out:

Harvest:

Successful varieties:

Comments:

Herb name:
....

Variety planted:
....

Seeds sown:
....

Germination period:
....

Seedlings planted out:
....

Harvest:
....

Successful varieties:
....

Comments:
....
....
....
....
....
....

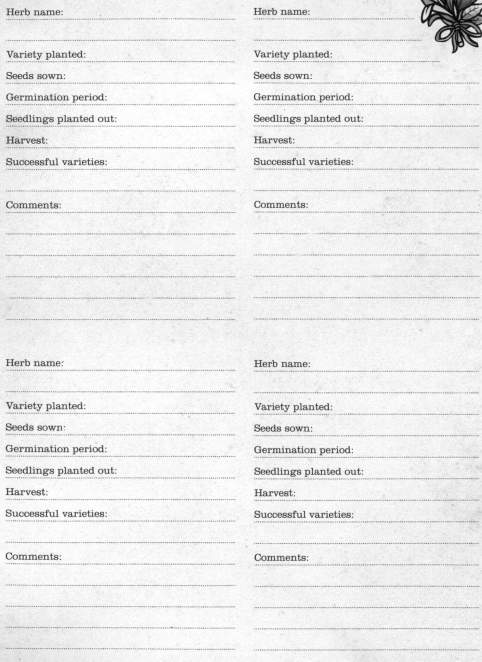

Herb name:
....

Variety planted:
....

Seeds sown:
....

Germination period:
....

Seedlings planted out:
....

Harvest:
....

Successful varieties:
....

Comments:
....
....
....
....
....
....

Herb name:
....

Variety planted:
....

Seeds sown:
....

Germination period:
....

Seedlings planted out:
....

Harvest:
....

Successful varieties:
....

Comments:
....
....
....
....
....

Herb name:
....

Variety planted:
....

Seeds sown:
....

Germination period:
....

Seedlings planted out:
....

Harvest:
....

Successful varieties:
....

Comments:
....
....
....
....
....

HERBS

Herb name:
....

Variety planted:
....

Seeds sown:
....

Germination period:
....

Seedlings planted out:
....

Harvest:
....

Successful varieties:
....
....

Comments:
....
....
....
....
....

Herb name:
....

Variety planted:
....

Seeds sown:
....

Germination period:
....

Seedlings planted out:
....

Harvest:
....

Successful varieties:
....
....

Comments:
....
....
....
....
....

Herb name:
....

Variety planted:
....

Seeds sown:
....

Germination period:
....

Seedlings planted out:
....

Harvest:
....

Successful varieties:
....
....

Comments:
....
....
....
....

Herb name:
....

Variety planted:
....

Seeds sown:
....

Germination period:
....

Seedlings planted out:
....

Harvest:
....

Successful varieties:
....
....

Comments:
....
....
....
....

Herb name:
....
....

Variety planted:
....

Seeds sown:
....

Germination period:
....

Seedlings planted out:
....

Harvest:
....

Successful varieties:
....

Comments:
....
....
....
....
....

Herb name:
....
....

Variety planted:
....

Seeds sown:
....

Germination period:
....

Seedlings planted out:
....

Harvest:
....

Successful varieties:
....

Comments:
....
....
....
....
....

Herb name:
....
....

Variety planted:
....

Seeds sown:
....

Germination period:
....

Seedlings planted out:
....

Harvest:
....

Successful varieties:
....

Comments:
....
....
....
....
....

Herb name:
....
....

Variety planted:
....

Seeds sown:
....

Germination period:
....

Seedlings planted out:
....

Harvest:
....

Successful varieties:
....

Comments:
....
....
....
....
....

NOTES

NOTES

NOTES

KEEPING ORGANIZED

Month 1

Week 1

Week 2

WEEK 3

WEEK 4

WEEK 5

Month 2

Week 1

Week 2

Week 3

Week 4

Week 5

MONTH 3

WEEK 1

WEEK 2

Week 3

Week 4

Week 5

Month 4

Week 1

Week 2

Week 3

Week 4

Week 5

Month 5

Week 1

Week 2

WEEK 3

WEEK 4

WEEK 5

Month 6

Week 1

Week 2

Week 3

Week 4

Week 5

Month 7

Week 1

Week 2

Week 3

Week 4

Week 5

Month 8

Week 1

Week 2

Week 3

Week 4

Week 5

Month 9

Week 1

Week 2

WEEK 3

....

....

....

....

....

....

....

WEEK 4

....

....

....

....

....

....

....

WEEK 5

....

....

....

....

MONTH 10

WEEK 1

WEEK 2

Week 3

Week 4

Week 5

Month 11

Week 1

Week 2

Week 3

Week 4

Week 5

Month 12

Week 1

Week 2

WEEK 3

WEEK 4

WEEK 5

NOTES

NOTES

Useful Contacts

Name:

Address:

Phone:

Email:

Name:

Address:

Phone:

Email:

Name:

Address:

Phone:

Email:

Name:

Address:

Phone:

Email:

Name:

Address:

Phone:

Email:

Name:

Address:

Phone:

Email:

Name:

Address:

Phone:

Email:

Name:

Address:

Phone:

Email:

Name:

Address:

Phone:

Email:

Name:

Address:

Phone:

Email:

Name:

Address:

Phone:

Email:

Name:

Address:

Phone:

Email:

USEFUL CONTACTS

Name: ....
Address: ....
....
....
....
....

Phone: ....
Email: ....

Name: ....
Address: ....
....
....
....
....

Phone: ....
Email: ....
....

Name: ....
Address: ....
....
....
....

Phone: ....
Email: ....

Name: ....
Address: ....
....
....
....
....

Phone: ....
Email: ....

Name: ....
Address: ....
....
....
....
....

Phone: ....
Email: ....

Name: ....
Address: ....
....
....
....

Phone: ....
Email: ....

Name:

Address:

Phone:

Email:

Name:

Address:

Phone:

Email:

Name:

Address:

Phone:

Email:

Name:

Address:

Phone:

Email:

Name:

Address:

Phone:

Email:

Name:

Address:

Phone:

Email:

USEFUL CONTACTS

Name:

Address:

Phone:

Email:

Name:

Address:

Phone:

Email:

Name:

Address:

Phone:

Email:

Name:

Address:

Phone:

Email:

Name:

Address:

Phone:

Email:

Name:

Address:

Phone:

Email:

Name:

Address:

Phone:

Email:

Name:

Address:

Phone:

Email:

Name:

Address:

Phone:

Email:

Name:

Address:

Phone:

Email:

Name:

Address:

Phone:

Email:

Name:

Address:

Phone:

Email:

Favorite Stores

Name: ....

Address: ....

....

....

....

Phone: ....

Email: ....

Comments: ....

....

....

....

Name: ....

Address: ....

....

....

....

Phone: ....

Email: ....

Comments: ....

....

....

....

Name: ....

Address: ....

....

....

....

Phone: ....

Email: ....

Comments: ....

....

....

....

Name: ....

Address: ....

....

....

....

Phone: ....

Email: ....

Comments: ....

....

....

....

Name:

Address:

Phone:

Email:

Comments:

Name:

Address:

Phone:

Email:

Comments:

Name:

Address:

Phone:

Email:

Comments:

Name:

Address:

Phone:

Email:

Comments:

FAVORITE STORES

Name:

Address:

Phone:

Email:

Comments:

Name:

Address:

Phone:

Email:

Comments:

Name:

Address:

Phone:

Email:

Comments:

Name:

Address:

Phone:

Email:

Comments:

Name:

Address:

Phone:

Email:

Comments:

Name:

Address:

Phone:

Email:

Comments:

Name:

Address:

Phone:

Email:

Comments:

Name:

Address:

Phone:

Email:

Comments:

Favorite Websites

Name:

Comments:

Name:

Comments:

Name:

Comments:

Name:

Comments:

Name:

Comments:

Name:

Comments:

Name:

Comments:

Name:

Comments:

Name:

Comments:

Name:

Comments:

Name:

Comments:

Name:

Comments:

Name:

Comments:

Name:

Comments:

Name:

Comments:

Name:

Comments:

Favorite Websites

Name:

Comments:

Name:

Comments:

Name:

Comments:

Name:

Comments:

Name:

Comments:

Name:

Comments:

Name:

Comments:

Name:

Comments:

Name:

Comments:

Name:

Comments:

Name:

Comments:

Name:

Comments:

Name:

Comments:

Name:

Comments:

Name:

Comments:

Name:

Comments:

Favorite Websites

Name:

Comments:

Name:

Comments:

Name:

Comments:

Name:

Comments:

Name:

Comments:

Name:

Comments:

Name:

Comments:

Name:

Comments:

Name:

Comments:

Name:

Comments:

Name:

Comments:

Name:

Comments:

Name:

Comments:

Name:

Comments:

Name:

Comments:

Name:

Comments:

Favorite Websites

Name:

Comments:

Name:

Comments:

Name:

Comments:

Name:

Comments:

Name:

Comments:

Name:

Comments:

Name:

Comments:

Name:

Comments: